This book is dedicated to the little kitchen scientists who like to mix and fix.

♥ PEL

Me on the Page Publishing
Copyright © 2024 Phelicia Lang M.Ed.

ISBN-13: 979-8-9855827-8-9

This book is sold subject to the condition that it shall not, by way of trade or otherwise, be lent, resold, hired out or otherwise circulated without the publisher's prior consent in any form of binding or cover other than that in which it is published and without a similar condition including
this condition being imposed on the subsequent publisher.
The moral right of the author has been asserted.

Illustrations Copyright © Phelicia Lang M.Ed.

Illustrations by Vicky Amrullah (Uzuri Designs)

TAY AND FRIENDS

Aleeyah Makes Playdough

By Phelicia Lang M.Ed.

Book 3

Dear Family,

Our world is filled with many fun things to explore, and your child is filled with wonder and amazement of how things work! Cultivate their interest by reading great books and providing opportunities for them to think like a Scientist, Technologist, Engineer or Mathematician.

This book will have challenging words as your child moves from **learning to decode the words**, to **reading to get information**. Little scientists will need to use non-fiction text skills to navigate the pages.

You can help them by using the strategy support graphics on the next few pages.

I'm sure they will say :"Hey, that's Me on the Page!" as they make connections while reading *Tay and Friends: Aleeyah Makes Playdough*!

Stay safe and Be Well,

Phelicia Lang

Learning to Read Strategies (K-2)

Look at the whole word 👀	math
Put your finger under the beginning letter of the word.	math 👆
Look for letter teams and patterns you might know.	ma(th)
Slide your finger from left to right slowly stretching out the letter sounds and teams in the word.	ma(th) →
Blend the sounds together to read the word.	ma(th) →

As they Read to Learn (2-5), think...

- Does my word make sense?
- Does my word look right?
- Does my word sound right?

Non-fiction Text Features in this Book	
### Label A word next to a picture that identifies what it is.	
### Keyword Important vocabulary words in the text that may be bold, italics, or colored.	These are my <u>safety goggles</u>.
### Glossary A page near the back of the book where you can find the meanings of the keywords.	 Experiment: pla that take place hypothesis

Chapter Headings A title or words before a chapter that tells you about the chapter.	
Caption A title or words underneath a picture that tells about the picture above it.	
Table of Contents A page in the front of the book that lists the titles and page numbers of the topics.	

Aleeyah Makes Playdough

Table of Contents

Chapter 1
Meet Aleeyah — 1

Chapter 2
Science Notebooks
& Lab Rules — 17

Chapter 3
Into the Lab — 21

Chapter 1
Meet Aleeyah

Hi! My name is Aleeyah.

I'm bright, bold, and beautiful. I dream of making things in the kitchen.

Mix it, fix it, shake it, bake it, Aleeyah knows how to make it!

A little bit of this.
A little bit of that.
Chemistry is where it's at.

My mom and dad are both scientists.

I spend a lot of time in labs.

My room is my dream space. This is where I think of ideas and look them up on my computer.

Looking for answers to find out more about something, or how to solve problems is called **researching**.

Look at my notebook. I keep it with me at all times.

My notebook is where I keep all of my science ideas.

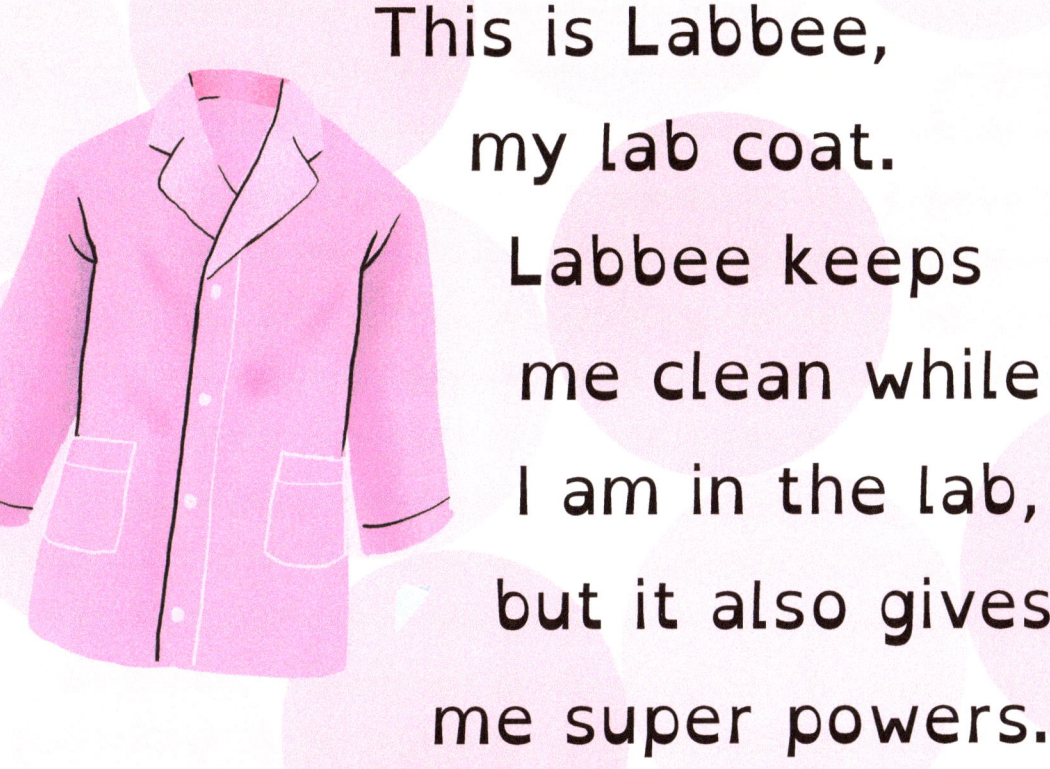

This is Labbee, my lab coat. Labbee keeps me clean while I am in the lab, but it also gives me super powers.

These are my **safety goggles**. I use them to protect my eyes.

Meet Cee-Cee 100, my computer.

Cee-Cee-100 is just like a good friend because I can ask her questions and she helps me find answers.

Did you know that cooking is really science? The science of mixing and heating things to see what happens is called **chemistry**.

Mix it, fix it, make it bake it. Chemistry is for me!

Stir it, whir it, let's see what it will be!

I love baking! I've helped my mom to make cookies, cakes, and pie crust.

I also love dough. I wonder how play dough is made.

Play Dough

Cee-Cee, how is play dough made?

Does it use flour like pie crust?

What keeps it from drying out?

How does the dough stick together?

Just like a real scientist she asks big questions and goes into the lab to find answers.

The family kitchen is Aleeyah's lab.

Deidre Gubac graduated from Tuskegee University with a Bachelors of Science in Chemistry. She went on to become a medical doctor. She played Doctor as a child and dreamed of taking care of patients. Her love of science, working hard, and helping people have helped turn her big dream into a reality.

Today her BIG question is:

What **ingredient** helps play dough to stay soft and squishy?

Aleeyah thinks it must be the oil. Her thinking or prediction is called a **hypothesis**.

She predicts the coconut oil will be the softest. When scientists ask questions, and test their answers, this is called an **experiment**.

Chapter 2
Science Notebooks & Lab Rules

My Science Experiment		
My Question:		
My Hypothesis:	vegetable oil (A)	coconut oil (B)
Method:		
My Results	vegetable oil (A)	coconut oil (B)

Aleeyah will do her experiment in the kitchen lab. Just like in a real lab, there are rules to stay safe in the kitchen:

1. Wash hands with soap and dry with a paper towel
2. Start with a clean workspace and tools
3. Wear safe clothes, such as goggles, and shoes. Put on a lab coat and gloves if needed.
4. Have an adult present
5. Use all equipment the right way
6. Keep all pets and animals out of the kitchen.
7. Clean up all spills right away
8. Stay focused

She will also wear the right shoes.

It's almost time to begin so she washes her hands and gathers all the materials needed.

Chapter 3
Into the Lab

Her friends came over just in time to do the experiment with her.

They all wash their hands! They put on safety goggles and lab coats next. Now they are all ready to begin.

Tay and Raj will test the play dough recipe with vegetable oil.

Aleeyah and Mari will experiment with coconut oil.

The Experiments

First, they measure the flour, salt, drink powder packet, and **cream of tartar** in a bowl. Then, they pour in the oils.

The kids must wait for Aleeyah's parents to pour the hot water into the flour mix.

Scientists observe what they see and make notes when they're in the lab.

It looks wet and sticky. Then it turns into a dough.

When it is cool, the kids will be able to **knead** the dough.

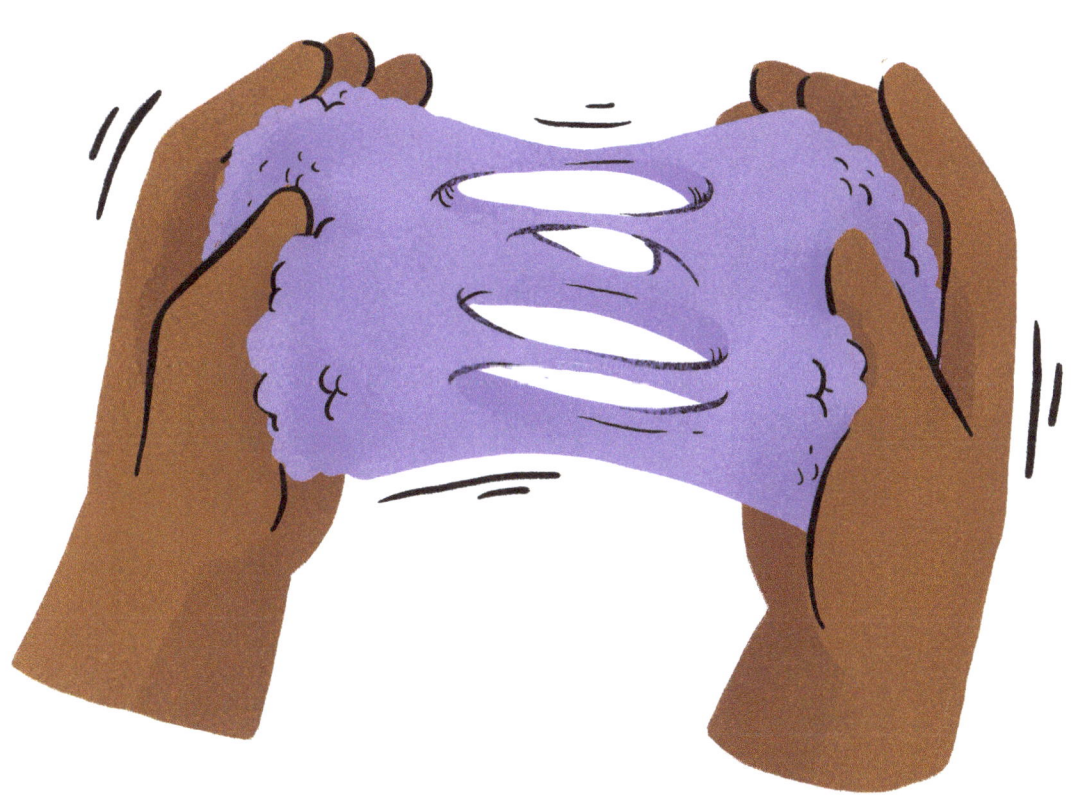

Tay and Raj's dough is still sticky and needs a little more flour to become **solid**. They both add a big pinch of flour to the dough. Now it is cool enough for the kids to **knead** the dough.

Tay and Raj have a red dough.

Aleeyah and Mari have a purple dough.

Both doughs are soft and smell good! The coconut oil dough is softer. Aleeyah's prediction was right!

Just like real scientist in a lab, they ask more questions.

What would happen if we used avocado or baby oil?

What ingredient could be added to make it even softer?

Aleeyah's mom tells them about glycerin that is used in soaps to make the skin soft. They will see if it makes the play dough soft too.

They take turns adding the ingredients while Aleeyah's mom mixes.

knead

When it is cool enough the kids knead it.

"This dough is the softest!", yells Mari.

"Ooh it's so smooth", says Raj!

OK Scientist, what did you find out from your experiments today?

"We learned that coconut oil makes a softer dough, than vegetable oil", said Tay.

"Glycerin will make any dough softer", said Mari!

"It is the SECRET ingredient", said Aleeyah!

Date		
Experiment	**A** (Tay/Raj) vegetable oil	**B** (Aleeyah/Mari) coconut oil
Hypothesis: my prediction is what I will test		Will be the softest
Method: (What I did)		
Observations		
Conclusion (What does it mean)		It is the softest

37

Date		
Experiment	**A** (Tay/Raj) glycerin	**B** (Aleeyah/Mari) regular recipes
Hypothesis: my prediction is what I will test	Will be the softest	
Method: (What I did)		
Observations		
Conclusion (What does it mean)	It is the softest	

Aleeyah and friends had a lot of fun in the lab today. What will you make?

Dear Young Scientist,

In Aleeyah Makes Playdough you learned the secret ingredient to making play dough soft and squishy. You also learned that the right amount of flour and liquid will make the dough more solid.

Did you know that the science of mixing ingredients and watching them react is chemistry. YES, chemistry!! Just like Tay and Friends, you are on your way to learning more about STEM (Science Technology Engineering Math).

You will do great things! Learning how things work and looking for answers to your questions is the secret to becoming a great scientist.

Stay curious and find the answers to your whys,

Phelicia Lang

Glossary

Experiment: plans or (actions) that take place in a lab to test a hypothesis

Lab: a place where experiments can be done in a safe and consistent way

Goggles: also known as safety glasses. They are used to protect the eyes from chemicals or objects.

Knead: the massaging, stretching, and folding of dough to make sure all of the ingredients are mixed well.

Observation: the act of carefully watching something

Prediction: a statement of what you think will happen

Method: a specific way or order of doing something

Hypothesis: a strong guess or feeling about what will happen in an experiment

Conclusion: the results or outcome of an experiment

Glycerin: is used in play dough to make it soft and keep it from drying out too soon

Solid: when an object is firm, not loose, and keeps its shape.

Cream of tartar: a dry powder made from grapes that is used in Play-Dough to make it more elastic.

Ingredients: one part of a mixture. When ingredients are combined they will form a mixture.

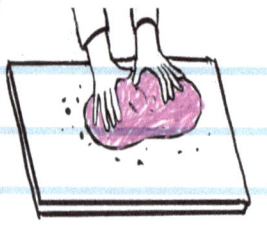

ALEEYAH'S KOOL-AID© PLAYDOUGH RECIPE

1 cup flour
1/4 cup salt
1-2 packets Kool-aid©*
1 Tablespoon cream of tartar
1 Tablespoon of oil
1 Tablespoon glycerin
3/4 cup boiling water

*2 packets will add more scent and color
*vegetable, coconut, baby, or avocado may be used. Use more if needed.

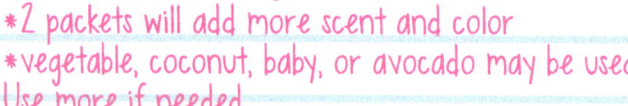

Instructions

1. Combine all dry ingredients in a bowl. Mix well.
2. With an adult, add the oils to the water and stir.
3. Slowly pour the water mixture into the flour mixture. Stir and mix well with a spatula. It will look very wet and sticky but allow 2-5 minutes to cool.
4. When cool enough, knead on a floured surface until mixed well with floured or oiled hands.
5. Please don't rush the kneading. The dough will be soft and stretchy when finished.
6. Store in an airtight container.

About the Author

Phelicia is a loving wife to Tony, and mother to four wonderful children, and precious grandchildren. They have all inspired her journey to find good books to reflect their lives and interests.

As a Reading Specialist, she's passionate about finding the right books to help readers connect to stories they love and books that reflect the readers.

Dreaming big dreams and using those dreams and gifts to help others, is the message she shares with her students.

When she's not creating on her computer she can be found Dreaming Big Dreams, reading and shopping.

What did you think of Aleeyah Makes Playdough?

Find my books on Amazon

If you liked this book, I'd love to hear from you. I hope you can take a little time to review it on Amazon.

Reviews help me to write better books and they help others to choose great books.

More Books by Phelicia Lang

Tay Book Series

Mari Book Series

www.meonthepage.com

www.ingramcontent.com/pod-product-compliance
Lightning Source LLC
LaVergne TN
LVHW070524070526
838199LV00072B/6695